6-Minute Messages
for Children

By Donald Hinchey

Loveland, Colorado

Dedication

To Alexis, a gift from God.

6-Minute Messages for Children
Copyright © 1993 Donald Hinchey

First Printing

Credits
Edited by Jennifer Root Wilger and Lois Keffer
Interior designed by Dori Walker
Cover designed by Liz Howe
Cover illustrated by Peter Pohle

Except where otherwise noted, scriptures are quoted from The Youth Bible, New Century Version, copyright © 1991 Word Publishing, Dallas, Texas 75039. Used by permission.

Library of Congress Cataloging-in-Publication Data
Hinchey, Donald, 1943-
    6-minute messages for children / by Donald Hinchey.
        p.   cm.
    ISBN 1-55945-170-X : $9.99
    1. Children's sermons. I. Title. II. Title: Six-minute messages for children.
BV4315.H514   1993
252'.53—dc20

                                                    92-42000
                                                        CIP
                                                        AC

Printed in the United States of America

Contents

The Creator: Messages for Knowing God

The Christian: Messages for Following Jesus

The Church: Messages for Life Together

Introduction

The great Swiss thinker Karl Barth will long be remembered for his many volumes of careful and complicated theology. Late in his life, when Barth was asked for a simple summary of his theology, he allegedly smiled and responded, "Jesus loves me. This I know. For the Bible tells me so."

The deepest truths of the Christian faith shine their brightest when they're presented plainly and simply. Jesus uses mustard seeds, shepherds and housewives, and the simple faith of children as models for life in the kingdom of God.

This sequel to *5-Minute Messages for Children* attempts to follow Jesus' example by presenting life in the kingdom of God in the most simple and active ways. Rather than requiring children to study the truths of the faith, these messages lead children (and eavesdropping adults) to experience and apply those truths to their lives.

Why Children's Messages?

Churches and other faith communities that regularly include children's messages in their worship and teaching hours have found that this brief time spent at eye level with God's little ones brings immense rewards:

● **Children learn and grow!** Children don't always learn the same way adults learn. Children's messages can teach important truths in ways kids understand.

● **Children are affirmed.** By setting aside five or six minutes to speak to our children, we let them know they're valued. Every children's message says implicitly, "You know, you kids are pretty important. We think you're great!"

● **The gospel takes on new meaning.** Children's messages challenge us to reshape and re-present the "old, old story" in a new package. Even adults will be refreshed.

Tips for Giving Children's Messages

Be Creative. The messages in this book aren't meant to be read. They invite creative innovation. Let them serve as catalysts for your own ideas. Don't be afraid to try new things. The children will forgive your failures and applaud your successes.

Prepare Well. Gather any necessary supplies beforehand and place them within easy reach. Mentally preview the message so you'll be able to anticipate children's responses—they may not always give you the answers you expect!

Get Down. Sit on the floor and look the children in the eye. Children's messages delivered by a big, standing adult can make children feel like they're being talked down to.

Speak Up. Use a microphone so the whole congregation can hear you.

Use Your Bible. Read the text for each message from your Bible. Encourage children and parents in your congregation to look up the text in their own Bibles at home.

Have Fun. You're sharing the good news! If you're enthusiastic with the children, the rest of the congregation will share in the excitement.

God bless you and your congregation as you embark on your adventure.

The Creator:
Messages for Knowing God

1. All Clear

Theme: Forgiveness

Bible Text: [The Lord says,] "I, I am the One who forgives all your sins, for my sake; I will not remember your sins" (Isaiah 43:25).

Preparation: You'll need five to seven hand-held calculators.

The Message:

Does anyone recognize this little machine? *Hold up a calculator and allow kids to respond.* That's right, this is a calculator. The calculator is a fantastic invention. You can use a calculator to add and subtract without counting on your fingers. Some friends have lent me their calculators for our message today. Does anyone here know how to work a calculator?

Several of the older children will hold up their hands. Invite them to take a calculator. Keep one for yourself and complete the following addition problems with the children.

Let's see if we can do some addition with these calculators. If you don't have a calculator, look on with a friend. *Pause while kids scoot together.* Let's add $3 + 3 + 4 + 4 + 5 + 6 + 7$. *Say the numbers slowly so kids can enter them as you speak.* What did you get? 32! That's what I got, too. Isn't this great?

How about $2 + 3 + 4 + 5 + 6 + 7 + 8$? What did you get this time? 35! Me too. Calculators make adding so simple.

Now let's add $7 + 9 + 4 + 6$. What did you get? *Kids will probably say "26."* You got 26? Oh my, I must have added wrong. I got 25. Here, I'll just push the "clear" button. Now I'll add it again. Yep. You're right. It **is** 26.

That little clear button is one of my favorite things about calculators. If you make a mistake, it just clears the screen and you can start all over again.

Read the text. The Bible says that God is the one who forgives all our sins. After we're forgiven, God won't even remember our sins. It's like God has a clear button for each one of us, and with just a touch of his finger, all our sins are gone forever.

Of course, we know it wasn't that simple. God sent his son Jesus to die for us, and that cost him a great deal. But because of Jesus' death and resurrection, all our sins are forgiven. God has wiped them away—just like I cleared my mistake on this calculator. We can start all over and never have to worry about the sins of the past.

Please return the calculators. Thank you for helping me today.

2. Weaklings

Theme: God's grace

Bible Text: But he said to me, "My grace is enough for you. When you are weak, my power is made perfect in you" (2 Corinthians 12:9a).

Preparation: You'll need a barbell or another object too heavy for a small child to move. Before the service, place the barbell in the center of the space where the children gather.

The Message:

Hmm! Someone has left this barbell right in our way. I do wish people wouldn't leave things laying around on the floor! *Choose a small, young child.* (Name of child), would you please move this barbell for us?

No matter how much the child tugs or pushes, he or she won't be able to move the object. After several tries, ask the child to come sit beside you.

Why can't (name) move this barbell? *Let children respond. Most will say the child is too small.* That's right. Children aren't strong enough to move heavy barbells. I shouldn't have asked (name) to move something that was too heavy. Let's all give (name) a big hand for trying to move the barbell!

We all try to do things that are too hard for us. No matter how hard we try to be good, we still do wrong things sometimes. But listen to what the Bible says about our weakness. *Read the text.* When we're too weak to be good on our own, God's power can help us. *Move the barbell.* God sent Jesus to take away our sins. Jesus moved the sin we were too weak to move, and he can help us become strong.

3. Umbrella

Theme: God's protection

Bible Text: Let me live in your Holy Tent forever. Let me find safety in the shelter of your wings (Psalm 61:4).

Preparation: You'll need two or three umbrellas. A sound-effects album with recorded rain and thunder would be a nice added touch.

The Message:

*I*f you've brought a sound-effects album, play it as children come up for the message. How many of you remembered your umbrellas the last time it rained? *Let children respond.* It seems that whenever I go outside, I always forget to take an umbrella. And then if it rains, I get wet. I brought a few umbrellas today to help us think about shelter and protection. Who'd like to put up an umbrella? *Pass out the umbrellas.*

Let's all get under an umbrella. *Give kids time to huddle under an umbrella.*

Umbrellas are so small and simple. You can put an umbrella in your car or briefcase; you can carry an umbrella to school or out to play. Then if it's raining, you stay nice and dry. Umbrellas come in all shapes and sizes—big ones you take to the beach to stay out of the sun or little ones you carry with you in case it rains.

Read the text. Psalm 61 compares God's care and protection to being under a tent. An umbrella is kind of like a tent you can take with you. No matter how hard it rains, we're warm and safe under God's umbrella. Wherever we go, we know we're protected by the umbrella of God's loving care.

Think of God's love as an umbrella, sheltering you from the storms around you. He'll always keep you safe. *Collect umbrellas.*

4. Baby Pictures

Theme: God's lifelong love

Bible Text: Lord, you are my hope. Lord, I have trusted you since I was young. I have depended on you since I was born; you helped me even on the day of my birth. I will always praise you (Psalm 71:5-6).

Preparation: After getting permission from some children in your congregation, ask their parents to bring one of their baby pictures to church. Bring one of your baby pictures as well. You'll also need two or three hand mirrors.

The Message:

I'm always surprised at how you can recognize people by looking at their baby pictures. I've asked some of the kids here today if it would be all right to show you their baby pictures and to see if you can guess who they are.

I'll show the picture, and you see if you can guess who it is. *Show three or four pictures, including your own. See if kids can guess.*

It's fun to look at our baby pictures and to remember what we were like when we were small. It might also be fun to look in the mirror and see how much you've grown. *Return pictures to their owners and pass around the hand mirrors.*

They didn't have cameras in Bible days, but one Bible writer remembered the time when he was young. Listen. *Read the text.*

When this writer remembers how God has been with him since he was a little baby, he's filled with praise. God has let you grow from little babies into wonderful kids. In just a few years you'll grow into teenagers and then adults. All along the way, God will be with you to love and care for you. We praise God for who you are and for who you will be!

5. Tears

Theme: God's comfort

Bible Text: The Lord God will wipe away every tear from every face (Isaiah 25:8a).

Preparation: You'll need an eyedropper and a small bowl of salt water.

The Message:

Do you ever cry? What makes you cry? When do you cry? *Let children respond.* I know I cry. Sometimes I cry at a sad movie or when I'm leaving someone I love. I also cry if I hurt myself or if someone hurts my feelings.

People cry for many different reasons. If we get something in our eye, tears wash it away. If we're hurt or sad, tears help ease the pain. If we miss something or someone, sometimes crying helps us feel better.

Jesus cried when he was sad, and he comforted his friends when they were sad. Tears are good for us, and we can cry when we're sad because we know God will take away our tears.

Listen to what the Bible says. *Read the text.* When the people of Israel were far from their homes, they cried because they missed their country and their families. But God promised that they'd soon go home. Then they'd be happy again. God would wipe the tears away.

God wants us to be happy. That's why he sent Jesus to die on the cross for us. But God also knows there are things that make us sad. When we're sad, tears can help ease the pain. Don't be afraid to cry. Even Jesus cried. But remember, God will always be there to wipe the tears away.

I would like to give each one of you a tear today. Not a real tear, but a reminder that God will wipe your tears away.

As the children leave, place a saltwater "tear" on each child's cheek with the eyedropper.

6. The Lost Is Found!

Theme: God's persistent love

Bible Text: "Suppose a woman has ten silver coins, but loses one. She will light a lamp, sweep the house and look carefully for the coin until she finds it. And when she finds it, she will call her friends and neighbors and say, 'Be happy with me because I have found the coin that I lost.' In the same way, there is joy in the presence of the angels of God when one sinner changes his heart and life" (Luke 15:8-10).

Preparation: You'll need a silver coin, brooms, flashlights, and a treat for each child. Hide the coin near the area where you'll be giving the children's message. Don't hide it too well! The children should be able to find it fairly easily.

The Message:

*P*ace nervously in front of the children. Continue pacing for several minutes or until one or more of the children try to get your attention.

Oh, I'm sorry. It's time for the children's message. I'm a little distracted today because I've lost something special. Have any of you ever lost anything? *Let children respond. Most will answer "yes."* Oh good, then you must know how I feel. I've lost a special silver coin, and I just can't seem to find it anywhere!

Would you mind helping me look for my coin? I have some brooms and flashlights here. Maybe if we all look for a minute, we'll find it.

Distribute the brooms and flashlights. Join the children in their search. When the coin is found, rejoice!

Oh, I'm so happy! We found my coin! Thank you for taking the time to help me look for it.

Jesus tells a story about a woman who lost a coin. Listen. *Read the text.* When we lose something that's important to us, we're sad. But finding it again makes us happy. God is like the woman who looked for her lost coin. Instead of looking for a lost coin, God is looking for lost people. God won't give up looking until he finds us. When God finds lost people, the angels in heaven rejoice. We can help God find lost people by telling our friends how much God loves them. And when God finds our friends, we can rejoice, too.

In Jesus' story, the woman invited her friends and neighbors for a party when she found her coin. I'd like to invite you to join me for some treats to celebrate the fact that God has found us. *Pass out treats.* Rejoice! God won't give up on finding lost people.

7. Through Dark Glasses

Theme: God knows all about us.

Bible Text: Now we see a dim reflection, as if we were looking into a mirror, but then we shall see clearly. Now I know only a part, but then I will know fully, as God has known me (1 Corinthians 13:12).

Preparation: You'll need several pairs of sunglasses, one for each child if possible. Bring a pair of sunglasses for yourself, too.

The Message:

*P*ut on your sunglasses as the children gather for the message. Raise your hand if you have a pair of sunglasses at home. Let's see, (name) has sunglasses and so do (name) and (name). Who's that sitting behind (name)? I can't see very well today. I wonder why? *Children will point out your sunglasses.* What? Oh, yes. I've forgotten to take off my sunglasses. *Take off your glasses.* That's much better.

I've brought a few extra pairs of sunglasses with me today. Would anyone like to try on a pair? *Distribute the sunglasses.* Now, let's see how you look. *Examine the kids in their sunglasses. Show kids to the congregation and then collect the glasses.*

I don't think sunglasses were made to be worn indoors. Why do people wear sunglasses? *Let children respond.*

Have you ever tried to guess what someone was thinking by looking into their eyes? You can usually tell if people are happy, sad, or angry if you look into their eyes. People say a lot with their eyes. Sometimes people try to hide their eyes behind sunglasses. They think that if they're wearing sunglasses, others won't know what they're thinking. Wearing sunglasses is like wearing a little disguise. The world looks different, and you look different, too.

Listen to what the Bible says about our disguises. *Read the text.* In this life, we can hide from other people. *Put on your glasses.* We can choose not to share our feelings. But when we're in heaven, we won't need to hide anything. *Take off the glasses.* God already knows all about us.

God wants us to be honest with one another. God doesn't want us to hide from one another. Just like God showed us his love and care by sending Jesus, God invites us to love and care for one another.

Sunglasses are good for keeping the sun out of our eyes. But we don't have to use them to hide from others. We don't have to use anything to hide from one another!

8. Whose Time Is It?

Theme: God's time

Bible Text: My times are in your hands (Psalm 31:15a, NIV).

Preparation: You'll need wristwatches, clocks, stopwatches, calendars, appointment books, and a marker. You'll also need a calendar to give to each child. Wear several wristwatches under your sleeve. *This is a good children's message for the Sunday closest to New Year's Day.*

The Message:

What time is it? *Allow a child with a watch to answer.* How did (name of child) know what time it was? How many of you are wearing watches today? *Let children respond.* Are any of you wearing the same watch? *Let children examine one another's watches before responding.* I brought my watch collection along today to show you some watches of different shapes and sizes. *Show the watches on your arm.*

What are some other ways people keep track of time? *Let children respond.* We keep track of hours and minutes with clocks and watches. *Show clocks and stopwatches.* Calendars and appointment books help us mark off days and months. *Show calendars and appointment books.*

People are funny about time. If we're doing something we enjoy, like playing with a friend or going to the amusement park, we never seem to have enough time. But if we're in a class at school or listening to a sermon at church, the time often seems to drag on and on. We keep looking at our clocks and watches to see how much time has passed.

People in Bible times didn't have watches or clocks. They didn't always know what time it was, but it didn't really matter. They were much more concerned about **whose** time it was.

Psalm 31:15 says, "My times are in your hands." All time is God's time—from the moment we get up in the morning until we go to sleep at night. And even while we sleep, God is watching over us and keeping us from danger.

If we remember **whose** time it is, then we won't always be so worried about **what** time it is. We can live every minute of our lives joyfully for God. *Take a calendar and a marker.* We're going to remember that (name of month) is "GOD'S" (name of month) and (name of day) is "GOD'S" (name of day). *As you speak, write "GOD'S" on the appropriate month and day.* God gives us each second and minute and hour and day. All our times are gifts to be unwrapped and offered back to God.

    I'm going to give each of you a calendar as a gift today. Starting with today, write the word "GOD'S" on each day this week—ask your parents for help if you need to. Try to remember not only **what** time it is but **whose** time it is.

9/97

9. Autumn Leaves
(A Back-to-School Talk)

Theme: Change

Bible Text: Praise God forever and ever, because he has wisdom and power. He changes the times and seasons of the year (Daniel 2:20-21a).

Preparation: You'll need baskets of fallen leaves or other autumn foliage to distribute to the children in your congregation. Before the message, gather the leaves into the baskets.

The Message:

I just love autumn! Autumn brings such beautiful changes to our world. The air is so crisp and clean. The leaves on the trees change color and sparkle in the sunlight. Then the leaves fall to the ground and make wonderful crackling noises when we step on them.

I've brought some autumn leaves with me today. *Pass the baskets around.* Each of you can take one or two leaves. It's hard to believe these leaves were once green and soft. The autumn sun and wind dry the leaves. The leaves turn the most beautiful colors.

Hold up a leaf. Hold your leaves in your hands and feel them. How do they feel? Smell the leaves. What do you smell? Look at the leaves. What colors do you see? *Let children respond.*

Autumn is a time of change. Just like these leaves, we're all changing in some way. I remember when some of you were too little to walk to the front for this children's message. You weren't in school and couldn't ride bikes. But now look at how grown up you're getting! I even see some teenagers in the congregation who once came up for these children's messages. They've grown up, too.

Growth and change are part of God's plan. Listen to what the Bible says about change. *Read the text.*

We'll never stay the same, and that's good. God wants us to grow and change! All along the way, God will be with us to guide and direct our change. Finally, when we're ready to die and leave this earth, God will change our bodies one last time and take us to heaven to be with him.

Keep your leaves with you this week. Each time you look at your leaves, give thanks to God for making change a part of his plan.

10. We've Got a Friend in High Places

Theme: God rules.

Bible Text: Then they said to each other, "Let's build a city, and a tower for ourselves, whose top will reach high into the sky. We will become famous. Then we will not be scattered over all the earth." The Lord came down to see the city and the tower that the people had built (Genesis 11:4-5).

Preparation: You'll need a stepladder with each step labeled "Money."

The Message:

Have you ever seen a skyscraper? *Let children respond.* Skyscrapers are pretty common today, especially in big cities. But in Bible times, buildings were usually much smaller. Many people lived and worked in tents. One time, some people decided to build a tall building. They wanted to be famous for building the tallest building around. As their building got taller, they thought they might like to try to get up into heaven where God lived. So they built higher and higher and finally had a building so high they were convinced they could get as high as God.

But they were wrong. The Bible says, "The Lord **came down** to see the city and the tower." No matter how high they built, God would always be higher!

Not all of us build skyscrapers, but sometimes we think we can get higher than God. *Walk to the ladder. Invite four children to help you.*

Some people believe that the more money they have, the greater they'll be. *Position a child on the first step.* What would you buy if you had a lot of money? *Let the child respond.* What about the rest of you? *Let other children respond.* Boy, that sounds like a lot of stuff. You might need some more money. *Position a child on the second step.* Now you should be able to buy everything you want with money to spare. Is there anything else you'd like to buy with your money? *Let the child on the second step respond and then ask for responses from other children.*

It seems like the more money you have, the more things you want to buy. You've used up your money again. *Position a child on the third step.* And what would you like to buy with your money? *Let the child on the third step respond.* I'm sorry, but you can't afford to buy that. *Position a child on the fourth step.* I bet (name of child on fourth step) could afford it though. (Name) has more money than all the rest of us combined!

Who gives us money? *Let children respond.* God knows we need money to buy the things we need to live. Money is a good gift from God. But we shouldn't use money to put ourselves above others or pretend to be like God.

We need to remember that no human being can ever be like God. Only God can be like God! No matter how high we think we are, God still has to come down to look at us. Jesus came down to earth in human form to love and save us. Jesus even came down lower than low. *Start taking kids off the ladder.* He showed us what it means to serve others by suffering and dying on the cross for us. Jesus doesn't want us higher than others—he wants us serving others. He wants us to remember that only God is above us all. We've got a friend in high places!

11. Why Are You Hiding?

Theme: You can't hide from God.

Bible Text: Then they heard the Lord God walking in the garden during the cool part of the day, and the man and his wife hid from the Lord God among the trees in the garden (Genesis 3:8).

Preparation: Choose three adult helpers prior to the children's message. Photocopy the list of excuses on page 25 and give one excuse to each helper. Before you begin the children's message, have your helpers hide in a place children can easily find. Have a microphone handy to interview your helpers once they're found.

The Message:

Do any of you like to hide from people? Why do you hide? *Let children respond.* We hide for lots of different reasons. We hide if we know we're in trouble or if we don't want to do something. We hide when we're afraid, and sometimes we hide just for fun, like when we're playing Hide-and-Seek.

I've asked some grown-up helpers to play a little hiding game with us today. Let's see if we can find them. *Divide kids into three groups.* When your group finds someone, bring that person up to the front of the room. After we've found everyone, we'll see if we can find out why they've been hiding.

Give kids several minutes to find the hidden helpers. Offer hints if they seem to be having trouble. When all helpers have been found, gather the group at the front.

Ask each helper the following questions: Who are you? Why are you hiding? *Helpers will each respond with the excuse you have given them.*

A long time ago, two people decided to try to hide from God. *Read the text.* Adam and Eve knew they had disobeyed, and they were afraid to tell God. So they tried to hide from God. But God found them, just like we found our helpers today.

God doesn't want us to hide when we're afraid. We can tell God anything, because God already knows our every action and thought. And God will always love us and forgive us, even when we disobey. There's no hiding from God!

EXCUSES

Who are you?

I'm (name of child)'s mother/father.

Why are you hiding?

I'm hiding because I don't want to make dinner. I'm afraid nobody will like what I cook.

Who are you?

I'm the (grade level) grade Sunday school teacher.

Why are you hiding?

I'm hiding because I don't want to prepare my lesson. I'm afraid it will be too hard for me and I won't do a good job teaching.

Who are you?

I'm a member of the choir.

Why are you hiding?

I'm hiding because I don't want to sing a solo. I'm afraid I'll get embarrassed and make a mistake if I have to sing all by myself.

12. The Last Laugh

Theme: God's victory

Bible Text: But the one who sits in heaven laughs (Psalm 2:4a).

Preparation: None

The Message:

Do you like to laugh? *Let children respond.* I love to laugh. What has happened to you lately that was so funny you laughed and laughed? *Let children respond. You might give an example of your own.*

If I tickled you, would you laugh? If I told you a silly joke would you laugh? When I count to three, let's all laugh together. Ready? One, two, three! *Lead kids in laughter.*

Hmm. That laugh doesn't sound very sincere. You can't fake laughter. It has to come from the heart. We laugh for different reasons, and each kind of laugh is different.

Pause after each of the following questions to allow children to demonstrate various kinds of laughter. How would you laugh if you heard a good joke? How would you laugh if I tickled you? *Tickle a child.* How would you laugh if you wanted to make fun of someone? How do bad guys laugh in the movies? How would you laugh if your feelings were hurt but you wanted to cover it up?

The Bible says that God laughs. It really does. *Read the text.* But God's not laughing because he heard a good joke or because someone tickled him. God laughs because it's so funny that people think they can be like God.

Sometimes people get so busy pretending to be like God they forget that only God is God. They think the world can get along without God's power. They think they have the right to tell other people what to do. They want to be forgiven but they don't want to forgive. They think death is the end and there's no heaven.

That makes God laugh. It's a real joke to think we can get along without God. God sent his Son to suffer and die for us, and then he raised Jesus from the grave. Jesus' resurrection was God's "last laugh." Because Jesus conquered death, we can laugh at sin and death and the devil forever and ever.

Let's have one last laugh with God. And let's remember that God always gets the last laugh!

Lead kids in laughter.

13. Crutches

Theme: God's empowering

Bible Text: Also, the Spirit helps us with our weakness. We do not know how to pray as we should. But the Spirit himself speaks to God for us, even begs God for us with deep feelings that words cannot explain (Romans 8:26).

Preparation: You'll need several sets of crutches and some canes. Also include walkers and a wheelchair if available.

The Message:

How many of you have ever had to use crutches? *Let children respond.* I've brought some crutches and canes with me today. Would anyone like to try them? *Pass out the crutches, canes, walkers, and wheelchairs. Let kids try them out.*

When we're hurt or our bodies aren't able to work on their own, we use crutches and canes to help us move around. I'm glad someone invented crutches. If we got hurt and didn't have crutches, we'd have to just sit around all day.

Sometimes people say believing in God is a crutch. What do you think they mean? *Let children respond.* Some people think that religion is only for people who are too weak to stand by themselves. But the Bible says we're all weak! Every one of us has been weakened by sin.

But God doesn't want us to stay weak. Listen to what God has done for us. *Read the text.* Through the Holy Spirit, God makes us strong. He holds us up and keeps us from falling. The Holy Spirit even prays for us when we don't know what to say.

Hold up the crutches. These crutches are pretty great—they keep people from falling. Our God is really great, too. He'll never let us fall.

The Christian:
Messages for Following Jesus

14. Leftovers

Theme: Jesus cares.

Bible Text: All the people ate and were satisfied. Then the followers filled twelve baskets with the leftover pieces of food (Matthew 14:20).

Preparation: You'll need several baskets and one or two large loaves of bread. Cut the bread into bite-sized pieces and place them in the baskets.

The Message:

How many people do you think we have in the church building today? 50? 100? 500? *Let children respond.* We certainly have a lot of people here. Jesus was once with an even larger group of people—5,000 men and many more women and children. These people had been talking and working all day, and they were getting hungry. Jesus' friends wanted to send the people away, but Jesus knew they were hungry. He fed all those people with just five loaves of bread and two small fish. It was a great miracle!

After the people finished eating, Jesus' friends took baskets and collected all the leftovers. *Hold up the baskets.* Their baskets were probably about the size of these baskets. How many baskets do you think they collected? *Let children respond.* The Bible tells us there were 12 baskets of leftovers.

Are any of you here hungry? Do you think anyone else in the congregation might be hungry? *Let children respond.* Maybe a few of these leftovers will keep our stomachs from growling during church! *Pass the baskets of bread around. When all the children have been served, ask several children to pass the baskets to the congregation.*

Jesus cares about hungry people. Although we may not be able to do miracles like Jesus did, we can help people who are hungry. There are hungry people in our own city and all around the world. We can show we care by giving some of our extra food to people who don't have enough. After church, ask your parents how your family can help.

15. Can You Write With Your Mouth?

Theme: Strength

Bible Text: I can do all things through Christ, because he gives me strength (Philippians 4:13).

Preparation: You'll need markers and paper.

The Message:

How many of you have to practice handwriting in school? *Let children respond.* I need four volunteers with good handwriting to help me with today's message. *Place children facing the congregation. Give each child a marker and a sheet of paper.*

Let's see you write "Jesus loves me" on your sheet of paper in your best handwriting. Be sure to use large letters so the people in the congregation can read your writing. *Pause while children write. When the children have finished, show the papers to the congregation.* You've all done a wonderful job! What beautiful handwriting!

Isn't it great that God has given us fingers and hands to use for writing? Some people aren't able to use their hands for writing. Maybe they've been involved in an accident or were born unable to use their hands. People who can't use their hands and arms for writing sometimes teach themselves to write with their mouths. Just for fun, let's see how you'd do if you had to write with your mouths. Put the pen between your teeth and try writing "Jesus loves me" with your mouth.

Allow a few moments for kids to try "mouthwriting." Monitor their progress, coaching them as necessary. From time to time remind them, "no fair using your hands." Collect supplies and continue with your message when kids begin to get frustrated.

Mouthwriting is hard, isn't it? Yet people who work hard at mouthwriting can actually write letters and books with their mouths!

One woman, Joni Eareckson Tada, even paints beautiful pictures with a paintbrush she holds in her teeth.

The Apostle Paul tells us that Jesus can help us do hard things. *Read the text.* Paul wanted to tell everyone about Jesus. That's a hard job. But Paul didn't have to do it alone. Jesus was with him, helping him do things that seemed impossible at first.

I'm glad we're able to write and draw with our hands. But if we couldn't use our hands, God would help us find other ways to write. God doesn't want us to give up and be sad when we can't do something. We can ask God to give us strength to use the abilities he gives us for his glory.

Do you remember the Bible verse I read earlier? Let's all say that verse together. *Lead kids in repeating the Bible text.* "I can do all things through Christ, because he gives me strength." Let Jesus help you with something hard this week.

16. Faith Like a Mustard Seed

Theme: Faith

Bible Text: Then Jesus told another story: "The kingdom of heaven is like a mustard seed that a man planted in his field. That seed is the smallest of all seeds, but when it grows, it is one of the largest garden plants. It becomes big enough for the wild birds to come and build nests in its branches" (Matthew 13:31-32).

Preparation: You'll need several small objects such as buttons or paper clips, a mustard seed for each child, and a large plant. Before the children's message, hide the small objects in the front of the sanctuary.

The Message:

What's the smallest object you can think of? *Let children respond.* I've hidden a few small objects here in the front of the church. Can you find them? *Allow children time to search for buttons and paper clips.* Who has the smallest object? *Let children compare objects until you find the smallest.* Jesus chose an even smaller object than this one to teach his disciples about God's kingdom. *Read the text.*

Pass out mustard seeds. I'm giving you each a mustard seed, and you'll see that it's very small. Roll it around between your fingers. It's one of the smallest seeds.

Sometimes our faith is as small as a mustard seed. Our little faith doesn't seem to do much good. But Jesus reminds us that this little mustard seed grows to be a great big plant—like this one. *Bring out the large plant.*

God can make a big plant grow from the smallest seed. All by itself, our little mustard-seed faith couldn't do much. But if we let God help our faith grow, we can accomplish great things for God's kingdom.

Give your mustard-seed faith to God . . . and look out!

17. Christian Yo-Yos

Theme: The Christian life

Bible Text: Since you were raised from the dead with Christ, aim at what is in heaven, where Christ is sitting at the right hand of God (Colossians 3:1).

Preparation: You'll need two or three yo-yos. If you can, invite someone skilled with a yo-yo to give a demonstration.

The Message:

Have you ever played with a yo-yo? *Let children respond.* When I was a kid, I used to play with yo-yos all the time. Would some of you like to play with a yo-yo while I'm talking? *Give yo-yos out to older kids.*

Each yo-yo looks a little different, but all yo-yos are made the same way. Let's look at our yo-yos closely. *Hold up a dangling yo-yo, string unwound.* This string is attached to a post inside the yo-yo. Let's wind up our strings. *Give children time to wind up their yo-yos.* When you hold on to your string and drop your yo-yo, the yo-yo spins up and down the string. Someone good with a yo-yo can make the yo-yo do great tricks as it spins. *Have your guest "yo-yo artist" demonstrate tricks for the children.*

This yo-yo reminds me of the Christian life. God puts us down on earth to do his will. *Spin the yo-yo down.* We spin around for awhile, but eventually we need God's power to keep on spinning. *Take the yo-yo up.* By prayer and worship we stay connected with God to get the strength and power to do God's will on earth.

Even though we're on earth, God wants us to aim for the things in heaven. *Read the text.* God wants us to remember that we belong to him. If we run out of strength down here *(let the yo-yo stop its spin)*, God reaches down and gathers us back up *(wind the yo-yo up)*. And one day God will take us up to heaven to be with him forever.

In the meantime, we Christian yo-yos keep spinning around, living on earth *(spin the yo-yo down)*, but always connected to God up in heaven *(take the yo-yo up)*. It's great being a Christian yo-yo!

20. The "Follow Me" Obstacle Course

Theme: Discipleship

Bible Text: My sheep listen to my voice; I know them, and they follow me. I give them eternal life, and they will never die, and no one can steal them out of my hand (John 10:27-28).

Preparation: You'll need three or four blindfolds and several objects to set up a small obstacle course. Ask one or two adult assistants to help you set up the course.

The Message:

*A*s you begin your message, have your assistants set up an obstacle course in front of the area where the children sit.
   Has anyone here ever gone through an obstacle course? *Let children respond.* Obstacle courses are used to train soldiers to run fast and to be quick and alert when they're on the battlefield. We've set up a little obstacle course here today. *Describe the course you've set up.* Could I have three or four volunteers to try my obstacle course? *Choose three or four children. Let them begin the course and then stop them.*
   Oh, I forgot to tell you. You have to do this obstacle course blindfolded. But don't worry, I'll lead you. *Have the volunteers hold hands. Then lead them through the obstacle course. Other children may call out directions or encouragement. When children have completed the course, remove their blindfolds and have them sit down.*
   There, we made it! Congratulations! *Lead children in applause for volunteers.*
   What would have happened if the blindfolded volunteers had to go through the obstacle course without a leader? *Let children respond.* Without a leader, they might have stumbled and fallen. The Bible says Jesus leads us like a shepherd leads sheep. Listen. *Read the text.*

39

When we're following Jesus, we can't always see what's up ahead. But if we listen to Jesus, he'll always lead us, just like I led our brave volunteers.

Of course, what happens in real life is a bit different from our obstacle course. When we're following Jesus, we don't reach the end of the obstacle course until we get to heaven. No matter how many obstacles are in our way, Jesus will always lead us through. And when we reach the end of our life, we'll be with Jesus forever.

21. The Pearl

Theme: Giving up everything for the kingdom of God

Bible Text: Also, the kingdom of heaven is like a man looking for fine pearls. When he found a very valuable pearl, he went and sold everything he had and bought it (Matthew 13:45-46).

Preparation: You'll need a string of pearls, a bag, and a tennis ball covered with shiny white paper. Put the tennis ball in the bag. Assign roles and have children act out the following story as you tell it. Add or subtract roles as necessary to fit the size of your group.

The Message:

*R**ead the text.*** That was a pretty short story, wasn't it? I wonder if we can add a few more details to it—then we can act it out. First we need a man. Who would like to play the man in this story? *Select a volunteer.* The man probably had a family—maybe a wife and a son. *Select children to play the man's wife and son.* They probably had a few pets, too—maybe camels. *Select two children to play camels.* This family probably lived in a house. *Select two children to "play" the house. Have them raise their arms to create a "roof" over the family.* This man probably worked in the marketplace, which was always full of people. *Form two groups with the remaining children. One group can form the walls of the marketplace, and the other group can mill around inside the "walls."* I think we're ready to perform our story now. Listen for your parts. When you hear your part, act out what you hear.

Once upon a time, there was a man named Jacob who bought and sold pearls. *Point out Jacob to your audience. Hand Jacob the string of pearls.* Jacob made a fine living with his pearls, and he lived with his wife, Rachel, and his little boy, Jonah, in a wonderful house. *Point out Rachel and Jonah. Give the "house" a small shake to show how solid it is.*

Every day Jacob loaded his pearls onto the camels and took them to the marketplace. *Pause while Jacob "loads" camels. Point out the market-*

place. Everyone in the marketplace loved Jacob's pearls. People far away could hear voices in the marketplace saying "ooh!" and "ahhh!" as people saw Jacob's fine pearls. *Have Jacob show the string of pearls. Pause for people in the marketplace to ooh and ahhh.*

Jacob believed that somewhere someone had the one Great Pearl. Jacob thought the Great Pearl must be so beautiful that he would be happy forever if he just looked at it. So as he bought and sold pearls, Jacob always looked for the Great Pearl. Every time he looked at another pearl, he would say, "It's not the Great Pearl."

And then one day he found it. *Give Jacob the bag with the tennis ball.*

Jacob ran home as fast as he could with the pearl in a bag. *Pause while Jacob runs home.*

"Oh, look, Rachel!" he exclaimed. "I found it! I found it! We'll be so happy forever and ever! Just look at it." *Have Jacob take the wrapped ball out of the bag.*

Jacob and his family oohed and ahhhed and touched the Great Pearl. *Pause for Jacob, Rachel, and Jonah to examine the ball.* Then Jacob said, "Well, we'd better get packed."

"Get packed?" Rachel and Jonah asked. *Encourage Rachel and Jonah to look perplexed.*

"Yes. You see, to buy the pearl I had to sell everything we have. The new owners of our house are coming in the morning. Our camels have been sold. *Lead camels away from the barn.* Our nice clothes have also been sold, and from now on we're going to be eating beans. But isn't this a great pearl?

Turn toward the marketplace. Now what do you think Rachel and Jonah did? *Let children respond. Then gather the group back together.* I think they were probably so excited about the pearl that they packed their suitcases right away.

Isn't that a great story? Let's give all the actors and actresses a big hand. *Lead the audience in applause.*

Jesus tells us that story so we won't forget that our life with God is precious. It's so precious that we would sell everything to keep it. God doesn't want us to have to sell everything, but we should always remember how precious God's love is. Jesus gave his very life so we could know God's love—the Pearl of great price.

22. Sand Living

Theme: Discipleship and the Christian life

Bible Text: Everyone who hears my words and does not obey them is like a foolish man who built his house on sand (Matthew 7:26).

Preparation: You'll need a bucket of sand and a large rock. Ask two strong adults to carry in the rock. Put down some paper or canvas to keep the sand off the floor.

The Message:

How many people here have ever played in the sand? Do you like playing in the sand? Why? *Let children respond.*

If you live near a lake or an ocean, it's fun to sit on the sandy beach and listen to the water. Or you can build a sand castle or just dig in the sand until you reach water. If you live near a sandbox, you can drive toy trucks around in the sand or build sand buildings.

But sand is not very good for building **real** buildings. Here, take a little bit of sand in your hand. *Pour some sand into each child's hand.* Why wouldn't we want to build a real building out of sand? *Let children respond. Most will probably say that sand is too soft or too light.*

Sand is soft and light, but sand also moves. If you build a house on sand and then the sand moves, what will happen to the house? *Let children respond.* It would be silly for someone to try to build a house on sand because the house would just fall down. *Read the text.* Jesus says if we hear his message and don't do it, we're just as silly as a person who tries to build a house on sand. Living our own way is "sand living."

Just listening to Jesus isn't enough. Jesus wants us to do what he says. Jesus says, "Love your neighbor," and we love them. Jesus says, "Feed the hungry," and "Heal the sick," so we take care of those people. When we do what Jesus says, we're building our lives on a very solid foundation. *Have the adult volunteers bring in the rock. Place your foot on it.* Just like this rock. This rock won't move like sand does. Let's do what Jesus says and live our lives God's way. That's "rock living"!

23. A Good Story

Theme: Evangelism

Bible Text: Jesus answered them, "Go tell John what you hear and see: The blind can see, the crippled can walk, and people with skin diseases are healed. The deaf can hear, the dead are raised to life, and the Good News is preached to the poor" (Matthew 11:4-5).

Preparation: You'll need a sign with a juicy bit of gossip written on it. For example, "Angie told Mary that she likes Jason, and Mary told Jason what Angie said." Make up your own "gossip" to fit the kids in your group, but don't use kids' real names.

The Message:

What is gossip? *Let children respond.* Gossip is spreading stories about other people that may or may not be true. Lots of people like to gossip. Why do you think people like to gossip? *Let children respond.*

Let's try a little fun gossip today. I'm going to ask several of you to make a line in front of us. *Choose several children to make a line.* Now I'm going to whisper a secret to the first person in the line. The first person will whisper it to the second person, and so on down the line. Let's see what the gossip turns out to be.

Whisper the secret to the first child, with the instructions to pass it on. As the children pass the secret along, walk behind the group and display the sign with the secret printed for the audience to see. Don't let any of the children see the sign.

When the secret reaches the end of the line, ask the last person to announce the secret to the whole audience. It will probably be different than what you've printed on the sign.

Here's the secret I told the first person in the line. We seem to get our gossip messed up, don't we? That's the problem with gossip—it can get confused. And when gossip gets confused, it can hurt people. That's why the Bible tells us not to gossip.

But there's a **good** way to tell stories. Jesus told John's disciples to tell others what they had seen and heard about him. And listen to the story they had to tell! *Read the text.* That's a good story, isn't it? We can tell others about the miracles Jesus did. We can spread the news about how much Jesus loves us—how he died for our sins and rose again, and how he wants us to be with him in heaven someday.

When we tell others how great Jesus is, we make God happy. That's not gossip—that's **good** news.

24. Fishers of People: A Mime

Theme: Evangelism

Bible Text: As Jesus was walking by Lake Galilee, he saw two brothers, Simon (called Peter) and his brother Andrew. They were throwing a net into the lake because they were fishermen. Jesus said, "Come follow me, and I will make you fish for people." So Simon and Andrew immediately left their nets and followed him (Matthew 4:18-20).

Preparation: You'll need an adult helper to be a mime dressed for fishing, carrying a fishing pole and a tackle box filled with different kinds of "bait." Your bait collection should include a dollar bill, a candy bar, a happy face drawn on a paper plate, a light bulb, and a large cross. You'll also need small crosses to distribute to the children at the end of the message.

The Message:

How many of you have ever been fishing? *Let children respond.* Fishing is a great hobby. The Bible tells us that Jesus' first disciples made their living by fishing. *Read the text.* I'd love to tell you more about fishing, but I don't have my fishing equipment with me. *The mime enters.* Look! Why, what a coincidence! Here comes a fisherman now. I guess we'll be able to hear more about fishing after all.

Hello, Mr. Fisherman. *The mime nods and waves to the kids.* We've just learned that some of Jesus' first disciples were fishermen. We'd like to learn more about fishing. Can you show us some of your fishing equipment? *Point out the fishing pole, the line, the hook, and the bait. Explain to the children how these things are used in fishing.*

We can fish for people today just like Jesus' disciples did. I wonder what kind of bait we'd use to catch people? I don't think very many of us would want to bite into a worm!

The mime looks into the tackle box, shrugs, and then holds up the dollar bill and begins to attach it to the line. Money? You think we could catch people for Jesus by offering them money? What do you think, kids? *Let children respond.*

I don't think money will work. What other kinds of bait do you have in your tackle box?

The mime looks into the tackle box, pulls out a candy bar, and begins to attach it to the line. Candy? I know kids like candy, but too much candy can make a person sick. Do you think people would come to Jesus if we offered them candy? *Let children respond.*

I'm sorry, but candy won't work either. *The mime frowns.* What else do you have in your box?

The mime thinks for a moment and then smiles and pulls out the paper plate happy face.

A happy face? You think people would come to Jesus if we promised that they'd always be happy? Maybe. But I don't think we should make people that promise. We might not be able to keep it. What do you think, kids? *Let children respond.*

So far, our bait supply won't catch many people. Do you have anything else in your box?

The mime holds the light bulb over his or her head to signify an idea and then pulls out the large cross and attaches it to the line.

The cross! Of course! God uses the cross to bring people to Jesus. God loves us so much that he sent his only Son to die for us. If we believe in Jesus, when we die we'll go to live with him forever.

The cross is the only bait that will really catch people for Jesus. When we tell others that Jesus loved us so much he was willing to die for us, they'll want to get caught! *The mime looks very proud.*

Do you think our friend has any more of that bait? *The mime looks into the tackle box and then pulls out the small crosses.* Let's each take one of these little crosses home this week. Use your cross to tell a friend about Jesus' love. Then you'll be a fisher of people, too.

Distribute the small crosses.

25. Lights of the World

Theme: Witnessing

Bible Text: You are the light that gives light to the world. In the same way, you should be a light for other people. Live so that they will see the good things you do and will praise your Father in heaven (Matthew 5:14a, 16).

Preparation: You'll need matches, a candle, a cigarette lighter, flashlights, a light bulb, and a helper to turn the overhead lights on and off.

The Message:

Have you ever thought of yourself as a light? *Let children respond.* Jesus says you're a light. Listen. *Read the text.* Jesus knows we live in a dark world, so he sends his followers out to brighten the darkness.

I've brought some different kinds of lights today, and I'd like you to think about what kind of light you might be.

Turn off the lights and strike a match. This match can create lots of light even though it's very small. But matches burn out quickly. *Turn on the lights.*

Light a candle and turn off the lights. Candles are better than matches because they last longer. But eventually candles flicker out, too. Some people's lights are like candles. They burn for a while and give off good light, but then they flicker out. *Blow out the candle and turn on the lights.*

Light the lighter and turn off the lights. I like this kind of light. You can carry a lighter around in your pocket, so its light is always available. But a lighter isn't a very dependable source of light. The light from a lighter comes on, then goes off. *Release the lighter. Flick it on and off a few times.* Some people's lights are like lighters that keep flickering on and off. *Turn on the lights.*

Turn on the flashlight and turn off the lights. Maybe your light is like this flashlight. We carry flashlights into dark places or when we need to look for something that we've lost. If you think your light is like a flashlight, you'd better keep a good supply of batteries!

Hold up a light bulb. Here's a wonderful kind of light. We can turn this light on and off with the flip of a switch. *Turn the lights off and on.* But light bulbs can burn out, too.

All of these different kinds of lights are important. But all of them have to be connected to a power source. And eventually they'll all burn out.

When Jesus asks us to give light to the world, he also promises to be our power source. Our lights will never burn out because they're powered by Jesus. People will see our light when we show our love to God and to others, and they'll want to praise God.

Your light may be small *(hold up a match)* or your light may be large *(hold up a flashlight or a light bulb)*. But no matter what kind of light you are, your light is powered by Jesus' love. And Jesus' love will never burn out!

26. Keys to the Kingdom

Theme: Eternal life

Bible Text: I will give you the keys of the kingdom of heaven; the things you don't allow on earth will be the things that God does not allow, and the things you allow on earth will be the things that God allows (Matthew 16:19).

Preparation: You'll need a large set of keys for the children to pass around. If you don't have many keys of your own, use the keys to the church. If you'd like to give the children souvenir keys, collect old keys from members of your congregation and put them in a box.

The Message:

I have a whole bunch of keys here. *Pass around the large set of keys.* I have keys to cars and homes, garages, and storage sheds. I also have some desk keys. I might even have a locker key. Keys are very important. Does anyone know why? *Let children respond.*

We use keys to lock things up. Sometimes we lock things up to protect them from rain or bad weather, like when you put your bike in the garage or the storage shed. We lock our houses so our things won't get stolen. Locks and keys are one way we keep things safe.

Jesus once told his disciples about keys. *Read the text.* Believing that Jesus died on the cross and rose again is our key to heaven. Jesus gives us the key to heaven so we can be with him forever. When we tell other people about Jesus and his great love for them, we're giving them the key to heaven's gates.

If you have a key for each child, continue the message. If not, let children return to their seats.

I'd like each of you to pick a key from my box. *Pass the box of keys around and let kids each select a key.* Carry your key with you to school this week. Keep it in your pocket or, better still, put your key on a string around your neck. Each time you see your key, remember to tell a friend about Jesus. Help someone else find the key to the gates of heaven!

27. A Bag Full of Goodies

Theme: Sharing

Bible Text: Then Jesus told this story: "There was a rich man who had some land, which grew a good crop. He thought to himself, 'What will I do? I have no place to keep all my crops.' Then he said, 'This is what I will do: I will tear down my barns and build bigger ones, and there I will store all my grain and other goods. Then I can say to myself, "I have enough good things stored to last for many years. Rest, eat, drink, and enjoy life! " '

"But God said to him, 'Foolish man! Tonight your life will be taken from you. So who will get those things you have prepared for yourself?'

"This is how it will be for those who store up things for themselves and are not rich toward God" (Luke 12:16-21).

Preparation: You'll need a bag full of goodies for each child, plus one or two extra bags to empty in front of the children. Fill your bags with candy, balloons, toys, children's books, or other small giveaway items.

The Message:

What am I going to do with all these goodies? *Empty a bag of goodies and sift its contents through your fingers.* I have so many goodies that I've run out of space. I don't know what I'm going to do!

I suppose I could build a bigger house to store my goodies. But building a house costs a lot of money. Maybe I could add on to my office, but that would cost the people in the church money. I know! What if we buried the goodies? We could take shovels out to the lawn and bury them in the dirt. Is that a good idea? *Let children respond.* Oh, it's so awful having so many goodies with no place to store them. What should I do? *Let children respond. They will probably suggest that you share your goodies. If no one suggests sharing, offer the idea yourself.*

Of course—I can share these goodies! Then I won't have to store them. We'll save lots of time and money, too! *Invite children to collect items from the bag you emptied.*

Jesus told a story about a man who had too many goodies. We sometimes call the man in the story the "rich fool." He was foolish because he thought he'd be happy if he had lots of things. Listen. *Read the text.* When the man reached the end of his life, he had to leave all his goodies behind. He was left with nothing, and it was too late for him to share.

Jesus knew about sharing. He shared his love and his power, and finally he gave away his life on a cross. Jesus would like us to share what we have, too. Many people in the world don't have clothes to wear or enough food to eat. We can help those people by sharing what we have. We can also help our friends by sharing with them. Sharing makes Jesus happy, and it makes us happy, too. Besides, if we share, we won't have to build bigger houses and barns.

I'm so happy that I can share my goodies with you today! *Distribute goodies to the children.*

28. The Fort

Theme: Including others

Bible Text: You were all baptized into Christ, and so you were all clothed with Christ. This means that you are all children of God through faith in Christ Jesus. In Christ, there is no difference between Jew and Greek, slave and free person, male and female. You are all the same in Christ Jesus (Galatians 3:26-28).

Preparation: You'll need one or two large folding tables, a large sheet or blanket, a microphone, and a bowl of treats. Before the message, drape the sheet or blanket over the tables to create a covered fort in which the children can hide. Hide the bowl of treats behind the fort.

The Message:

How many of you have ever built a fort? *Let children respond.* I've noticed that children like to build forts. A fort is a special place for kids. You can have secret meetings and special treats in a fort. And moms or dads or certain other kids usually aren't invited.

I've built my own fort today, and I'd like to invite some of you to come inside. I only have room for (X) kids, so some of you won't be able to come in. Sorry about that. Let's see—who should I invite? *Choose (X) kids at random.* I'm sorry but the rest of you will just have to wait here while we go into my special fort.

Lead the children you have chosen into the fort. Take your microphone in with you so the audience can hear your voice from under the table.

Well, here we are. Aren't you glad you got invited into my fort? *Let children respond.* It's certainly dark in here. Did anyone remember to bring a flashlight? No? Well, it's still fun. Where are the treats? Did anyone remember the treats? No? Well, I'm sure we can have fun without treats. What? You're hot? Yes, it's a little crowded in the fort. But just think how lucky you are to be in my fort. Some kids didn't even get to come in.

Pause for a moment. What? You don't want to be in here anymore?

But I invited you into my fort. Don't you feel special? *Let children respond.* Well, I sort of miss the rest of the kids, too. Maybe we should go outside. *Lead children out of the fort.*

Whew! We were a little squashed inside my fort, and I missed all of you kids out here. I guess being in my fort wasn't as nice as we thought it would be.

In Paul's time, some Christians thought they were better than others. So they built a kind of fort to keep the others out. But Paul wrote them a letter to remind them that Jesus died for everybody. *Read the text.*

God doesn't want us hiding in forts. God invites all people to come into his kingdom, not only people just like us. In God's kingdom we all enjoy one another's special gifts together. And that's better than hiding away in some dark fort any day!

Let's pray. *Encourage children to bow their heads.* Dear God, we thank you for giving us so many different kinds of people to be in your kingdom. We thank you for men and women, boys and girls, old people and young people of every race and nation. Help us to welcome everyone into your kingdom and your church. Amen.

Now, let's all have some treats! *Distribute treats to the children.*

29. The Good Sheep Dog

Theme: Caring

Bible Text: The Lord is my shepherd, I have everything I need (Psalm 23:1).

Preparation: You'll need a large picture of a sheep dog.

The Message:

How many of you know the 23rd Psalm? *Let children respond.* The 23rd Psalm begins like this. *Read the text.* Sometimes we call the 23rd Psalm "The Good Shepherd Psalm" because it teaches us that God is like a shepherd and we're like sheep. But the 23rd Psalm doesn't mention sheep dogs.

I've brought a picture of a sheep dog with me today. *Show children the picture.* We aren't told if sheep dogs were used in Bible times. But today it's very common for shepherds to have sheep dogs. What does a sheep dog do? *Let children respond.*

Let's do a little play about sheep dogs. We'll call it "A Day in the Life of a Sheep Dog." *Point to the whole group of children.* We'll pretend that all of you are sheep. (Name of child) and (name of child) will be sheep dogs. (Name of child) can be a fierce wolf. *Point to an area several feet away from the group.* Why don't you stand over there, fierce wolf?

I'll be the director. Listen to my instructions so you'll know what to do. Since you're all playing animals, you'll need to get down on your hands and knees. *Pause while children get into position.*

One day a flock of sheep was grazing quietly in the meadow baaing softly. *Encourage children to baa.* Suddenly, one of the sheep began to wander away from the flock. *Motion to one child to move away from the flock.*

Right away the sheep dogs noticed someone was missing. The sheep dogs began to bark and ran after the missing sheep. *Point to the sheep dogs and encourage them to bark.* The sheep dogs kept on barking until the little sheep went back to the flock. *Motion to the lost sheep to return to the group.*

Another day a fierce wolf appeared. The wolf growled and howled at the sheep. *Encourage the fierce wolf to growl and howl.* The sheep dogs ran right up to the wolf and barked loudly to scare it away. *Pause to allow the sheep dogs to scare the fierce wolf away.*

Thanks to the sheep dogs, the sheep could go back to their grazing and baaing. *Encourage sheep to graze and baa.* Let's give our sheep, sheep dogs, and fierce wolf a big hand! *Lead the audience in applause as you call the children together.*

We're all God's sheep, and Jesus is our Good Shepherd. But sometimes God needs us to be sheep dogs. When God's sheep start to wander away, God wants us to remind them of his love and care. When members of God's flock are in trouble, God wants us to help them. God needs good sheep dogs to help care for his sheep. Be a good sheep dog this week and remind people how much God loves them!

30. Make the Weak Hands Strong

Theme: Supporting the weak

Bible Text: Make the weak hands strong and the weak knees steady (Isaiah 35:3).

Preparation: You'll need a simple splint. You can make your own out of two boards and long strips of cloth. Before the message, ask two children to help you.

The Message:

One day a group of children from a church went for a hike in the mountains. *Motion for children to follow you.* The children walked up a long path into the hills where the trees grew tall and the grass was high. *Lead children up and down the center aisle of the sanctuary.*

After a while, (name of child) and (name of child) got tired of walking. Even though their leader had warned them not to, (name) and (name) started pushing and shoving. *Motion for your helpers to gently shove each other.* (Name of first child) shoved (name of second child) and then ran away through the high grass.

Suddenly, the kids heard a sharp cry. When they turned to look, (name of first child) had disappeared into the grass. The group hurried to look for their friend. When they found (name), (name) was rolling in the tall grass, holding his/her knee. *Have one of your volunteers groan and hold his or her knee.* (Name)'s face was twisted in pain. "I stepped in a gopher hole," (name) groaned.

The children and their leader bent down to examine (name)'s knee. *Gather children around the "injured" child.* "It looks like a bad twist," the leader said. "We'd better make a splint."

They found two boards by the side of the path. *Take out the boards and the strips of cloth. Have your "injured" volunteer stretch out one leg.*

Attach the "splint" to the leg by wrapping the cloth around the two boards. They tied the boards tightly around (name)'s knee and helped (name) walk back to the road. *Lead children back to the children's message area. Encourage them to help (name) walk.* Then their leader drove (name) to a hospital. The children learned a painful lesson about careful hiking that day.

You all did a great job helping (name) walk. Listen to what the Bible says about helping people who are hurt or weak. *Read the text.* We all have times when we're hurt or weak and need help. God wants us to watch out for one another. When others around us fall, God wants us to help them up.

We're all in this life together. When we give to the poor, visit a sick friend, or just listen to someone who's sad, we're helping people up. And someday if we fall and lose our strength, our friends will be there to help us up. God gives us strength to help one another!

31. Move Up Higher

Theme: Humility

Bible Text: So when you are invited, go sit in a seat that is not important. When the host comes to you, he may say, "Friend, move up here to a more important place." Then all the other guests will respect you (Luke 14:10).

Preparation: You'll need metal folding chairs and a bag of candy, small toys, or other goodies. Line up the folding chairs in a single line. Stand at one end of the line with the bag of goodies.

The Message:

How many of you have ever been invited to a party? *Let children respond.* Jesus once told a story about going to a party. When you go to a party today, it doesn't matter where you sit, but in Jesus' day certain people had special seats. I'd like (X) volunteers for a party. Who'd like to come? *Choose enough children to fill the chairs you've set up.*

When I say "go," I want each of you to sit in a chair. When everyone is seated, I'll let you each choose one of these presents. The children sitting closest to me will get to choose their presents first. Ready? Go! *The children will scramble for the chairs closest to you.*

Now I'll let you choose your presents. But first, I have to do one thing. *Pick up the bag of goodies and walk to the other end of the line. Invite the children to turn their chairs to face you.*

Begin to shuffle through your bag of goodies. Shall we choose our presents now? *Let children respond. The children who are now seated farthest from you will protest.*

I played a little trick on you, didn't I? Everyone likes to be first in line. But listen to what Jesus told his friends about being first. *Read the text.* Everyone likes to win. You wouldn't want to join a team if you knew the team was going to lose. We all want to be first.

But Jesus tells us that being first isn't the most important thing. Jesus' followers put others first. "The last shall be first; and the first shall be last," Jesus tells us. You may not like being last, but if you serve others you'll be first with Jesus in heaven.

Should I give these children their prizes now? Do you think my game was fair? *Let children respond.* I don't think my game was fair either. So I brought some nice surprises for all of you—even for the kids who didn't play. *Distribute goodies to the children.*

Thanks for helping me with today's children's message.

32. The Greatest Job in the World

Theme: Serving others

Bible Text: Jesus called them together and said, "The non-Jewish people have rulers. You know that those rulers love to show their power over the people, and their important leaders love to use all their authority. But it should not be that way among you. Whoever wants to become great among you must serve the rest of you like a servant. Whoever wants to become the first among you must serve all of you like a slave. In the same way, the Son of Man did not come to be served. He came to serve others and to give his life as a ransom for many people" (Mark 10:42-45).

Preparation: You'll need a chalkboard eraser, a bandage, a bottle of spray cleaner, and a pot.

The Message:

I've brought a few things with me today that people might use in their jobs. Let's see if we can guess what their jobs are.

Hold up the chalkboard eraser. Now who would use an eraser? Someone who writes on the chalkboard a lot. Who might that be? *Let children respond. Then hold up the bandage.* Who do you think uses a bandage to do a job? *Let children respond. Then hold up the bottle of spray cleaner.* Our church uses this bottle of cleaner to clean the tables in your Sunday school rooms. Who else might use a bottle of cleaner? *Let children respond. Then hold up the pot.* How many of you have ever seen your mom or dad cook in one of these? Who else would use a pot? *Let children respond.*

These are just a few of the jobs people do. When you grow up, you'll all have jobs, too. If you could have any job in the whole world, what job would you want? What's the greatest job in the whole world? *Let children respond.*

Jesus says serving others is the greatest job of all. *Read the text.*

Jesus spent his whole life serving others, and he wants us to serve others, too. We can all help one another in so many different ways. Can you name the people who have served you this week? *Let children respond. Remind them to include parents, teachers, and church workers.* What are some things you can do to serve others? *Let children respond.*

Remember, when you're serving others you're doing the greatest job in the whole world!

33. The Leap of Faith

Theme: God's help

Bible Text: So don't worry, because I am with you. Don't be afraid, because I am your God. I will make you strong and will help you; I will support you with my right hand that saves you (Isaiah 41:10).

Preparation: Tape two 4-foot strips of masking tape to the floor, 12 to 15 feet apart.

The Message:

How many of you like to jump? *Let children respond.* Let's see how high you can jump. *Let the children practice their jumps.* What about jumping a long distance? How far can you jump? How many of you think you can jump 1 foot? What about 2 feet? *Line the children up along one strip of tape and let them jump as far as they can.*

How many of you think you can jump from this piece of tape to that piece of tape across the room from us? Let's see. *Let the children jump across the room and back.* Now, how many of you can jump to that other piece of tape in one jump?

Choose one of the smallest children in the group. I bet (name of child) can jump that far. Watch! *Pick up the child under the arms and carry him or her across to the other tape strip.* Wow! What a great jump! Isn't (name) a great jumper? *Let children respond. Most will probably complain that the jump wasn't fair.*

Every one of us would need help to make a jump this big. Our faith is kind of like the jumping game we've been playing today. There are some things we just can't do by ourselves. We have to trust God to help us. *Read the text.* God promises to support us just like I supported (name). When we're feeling weak, we can just jump into God's arms, and he'll help us be strong.

Let's each take one more leap of faith before we return to our seats.

The Church:
Messages for Life Together

34. Intertwined

Theme: The body of Christ

Bible Text: Together you are the body of Christ, and each one of you is a part of that body (1 Corinthians 12:27).

Preparation: Give kids each a 3-foot piece of string as they arrive at the worship service. Keep a piece of string for yourself. Ask the children to bring their strings with them to the children's message.

The Message:

Y ou were each given a piece of string when you came in today. Does everyone have a piece of string? *Make sure all the children have a piece of string.* What can you do with your piece of string? *Let children respond.*

What would happen if we joined our pieces of string? Tie your piece of string to someone else's. Let's see how long a rope we can make. Perhaps some of you older children can help the younger ones. While you're tying your strings together, I'll read a passage from the Bible. *Read the text.*

God has given each of us some pretty wonderful gifts. We can each use our gifts to do great things for God. But if we all join our gifts together, we can do so much more. That's one reason we have churches. A church is a group of Christians who put their gifts together to serve God and tell others about Jesus' love. *Tie your piece of string to the end of the rope.* When I join my gifts and abilities with yours, we all become stronger. Now, let's see how much our string has grown. *Have the children spread out and stretch the string to its full length.*

Have the children form a tight bunch and wrap the string around them. We are the body of Christ. God has joined us together to do wonderful things!

35. An Interview With a Foot

Theme: The church

Bible Text: The human body has many parts. The foot might say, "Because I am not a hand, I am not part of the body." But saying this would not stop the foot from being a part of the body (1 Corinthians 12:14-15).

Preparation: Place a large man's shoe on a chair where the children can see it. You'll also need an adult helper. Position your helper offstage, out of the children's sight. Give your helper a microphone and a copy of the following script.

The Message:

*R*ead the text. What a curious Bible verse! Can you imagine a foot not wanting to be a part of the body? *Let children respond.*
  Maybe we should all check our feet to make sure they're connected. *Give children time to check their feet.* Are all of your feet connected to your bodies? *Let children respond.* That's good. This foot looks like it might be disconnected. *Point to the shoe.* Let's see how this foot feels about being part of the body.
  Speaker: Good morning, Mr. Foot. Thank you for coming. *Extend your microphone toward the shoe each time you offer a question or comment.*
  Foot: *(adult helper offstage)* Thank you for inviting me.
  Speaker: Have you ever felt like not being a part of the body?
  Foot: Oh yes, many times. We feet aren't very pretty, you know. Hands are so delicate, and ears are so necessary. Mouths can sing God's praises, and noses come in so many shapes and sizes. But we feet are just... funny looking.
  Speaker: I think you're a good-looking foot!
  Foot: Not compared to the arm. The arm is so strong. Or the graceful neck or the noble chin. No wonder people keep me in shoes—they just don't like looking at me. And then there are those cruel comments about smelly

feet. That hurts, you know!

Speaker: But we need you, Mr. Foot! Don't we, kids? *Let children respond.* If it weren't for you, we wouldn't be able to walk or run or even stand up! We keep you in shoes to protect you because we need you so much!

Foot: Well...I don't know.

Speaker: We're all needed in the body. The Bible says so—we just read it. God gives each part of the body a job to do. The church is that way, too. Every person is important. And we all need each other.

Foot: Hmmm. Now that you mention it, I guess I am pretty important even if I don't always get the most attention.

Speaker: God needs every one of us to do his work. I'm glad you're a foot, Mr. Foot! Thanks for coming to visit us today.

Foot: Thanks for inviting me.

Have any of you children ever felt left out like Mr. Foot? *Let children respond.* Whenever you feel left out, remember our talk with Mr. Foot. We're all important to God!

36. The Church Band

Theme: Spiritual gifts

Bible Text: There are different kinds of gifts, but they are all from the same Spirit. There are different ways to serve but the same Lord to serve. And there are different ways that God works through people but the same God. God works in all of us in everything we do (1 Corinthians 12:4-6).

Preparation: You'll need three kazoos and a box of other rhythm instruments. Kazoos can be made by covering combs with waxed paper.

The Message:

How many of you know how to play a musical instrument? *Let children respond.* Today we're going to put those talents to work. We're going to start a church band. Every church needs a band. We'll start our band with three kazoos. Does anyone know how to play a kazoo? *Choose three volunteers.*

Let's begin by playing "If You're Happy and You Know It." *(You may want to choose another simple, familiar song.)*

After several measures, interrupt the children. Wait a minute! Something's wrong with our band. Everyone is playing the same instrument!

The Bible tells us about a church that had the same problem. All the people wanted to do the same thing. If anyone wanted to do something different, he or she was laughed at. Paul had some good advice for this church. Listen. *Read the text.*

Our gifts are like the instruments in a band—if everyone always played the same instrument, the music would be pretty dull. But when all the instruments put their different sounds together, they make beautiful music. When I look at you, I know that God has given each of you a different gift. *Look around the group and name some of the children's talents you know about.* God wants us to use our different gifts to help one another.

Let's see what we can do to improve this band. *Distribute the remaining rhythm instruments.* Now let's praise God together! *Lead children in a song.*

37. Keep It Up

Theme: Cooperation

Bible Text: And Christ gave gifts to people—he made some to be apostles, some to be prophets, some to go and tell the Good News, and some to have the work of caring for and teaching God's people. Christ gave those gifts to prepare God's holy people for the work of serving, to make the body of Christ stronger (Ephesians 4:11-12).

Preparation: You'll need a balloon for each child. Blow up five or six of the balloons.

The Message:

*H*old up a balloon. How many of you like balloons? *Let children respond.* I've brought a few balloons to give away. Who would like these balloons? *Select one child.* (Name of child), you may have all these balloons if you can just keep them up in the air for one minute. Do you think you can do that? *Let the child respond.* I'll throw the balloons into the air, and all you have to do is keep them up. The rest of us will cheer for (name). *Throw the balloons into the air and lead the other children in cheering. The balloons will fall before time runs out.*

That's too bad. I really wanted to give (name) my balloons. Maybe if we all help, we can keep the balloons in the air. Then everyone can have a balloon. Maybe our congregation will even cheer us on. Let's try that. Is everybody ready? Go! *Throw the balloons into the air and lead the congregation in cheering.*

When a minute has passed, call the children back to the message area. Read the text. God wants people in the church to work together—just like when we all helped keep the balloons in the air. God gives people many different kinds of gifts to help the church. Pastors and teachers have special gifts, but so do each of us. God needs us all to use our gifts. When we work together, we can accomplish great things for God's kingdom!

I'm going to give each of you a balloon to help you remember how much fun we had cooperating today.

38. What Do You Do With This Beautiful Book?

Theme: The Bible

Bible Text: All Scripture is given by God and is useful for teaching, for showing people what is wrong in their lives, for correcting faults, and for teaching how to live right. Using the Scriptures, the person who serves God will be capable, having all that is needed to do every good work (2 Timothy 3:16-17).

Preparation: You'll need Bibles in various translations, sizes, and shapes. Be sure to include a children's Bible in your collection. You'll also need a stack of papers and a small folding table.

The Message:

I've brought a wonderful book with me today. *Hold up a Bible.* Do you recognize this book? *Let children respond.* That's right. This is the Bible. Let me show you some of the ways people use the Bible.

Place a large Bible on the table. Lots of people have Bibles in their homes. They leave their Bibles on tables. Sometimes people use the Bible like a paperweight to keep papers from flying around in the wind. *Place the large Bible on top of the paper.*

Sometimes witnesses in trials are "sworn in" with a Bible. *Open a Bible and put a child's hand inside.* The bailiff asks the witness, "Do you swear to tell the truth, the whole truth, and nothing but the truth, so help you God?" *Turn to the child touching the Bible.* You would never tell a lie while you had your hand on the Bible, would you? *Let the child respond.*

I've also heard that the Bible has saved people's lives. *Put a small Bible in your shirt pocket.* During times of war, some soldiers kept Bibles in their pockets. When the soldiers got shot, the bullets went into their pocket Bibles, and they weren't hurt. Isn't that amazing?

Bibles make great gifts, too. If you don't know what to give for a gift, give a Bible! Bibles come in all shapes and sizes. *Show your Bible collection.* I know one more way we can use these Bibles. What do you think it is? *Let children respond.*

We can read the Bible! Lots of people have Bibles in their homes, but not everyone reads the Bible. Listen to what Paul told his friend Timothy about the Bible. *Read the text.*

The Bible is God's gift to us. But like any gift, the Bible doesn't do much good unless we use it. Paul says we can use the Bible for teaching and for helping one another live God's way. The Bible tells about God's great love for Israel and for all people. The Bible tells us how Jesus was promised and how he came to teach and serve, to suffer and die, and then to rise again. The Bible is a great book. But it won't help you unless you read it.

Reading the Bible is sometimes hard for children. But your moms and dads can help you pick out a Bible that's just right for you to read. *Show the children's Bible.*

The Bible makes a beautiful paperweight, and in court it helps people remember to tell the truth. But the Bible is God's gift to us. So let's read it!

39. Bubbles

Theme: God's Word

Bible Text: The grass dies and the flowers fall, but the word of our God will live forever (Isaiah 40:8).

Preparation: You'll need a bubble wand and a bottle of bubble soap. Make sure the soap is nonstaining if you're giving the children's message in a carpeted area.

The Message:

It's so much fun to blow bubbles. Watch this! *Blow some bubbles.* Aren't they pretty? Does anyone else want to blow some bubbles? The rest of us can try to catch the bubbles. *Let several children try blowing bubbles.* Bubbles are wonderful because they're so pretty. But bubbles are kind of sad, too. Bubbles don't last long. They pop, and then they're all gone.

Read the text. The Bible says that nothing on earth will last forever. The grass and flowers may last longer than a bubble, but after a while they die, too. Even people have to die someday. The Bible says that only God's Word will last forever.

Jesus is God's living Word. Jesus came into this world to give us a life that lasts forever. We know that when we die we won't disappear like a bubble. We'll go to heaven to be with Jesus. Because Jesus died and rose again, we'll live forever.

Blow a few more bubbles. Bubbles are fun and pretty. But they don't last. God's Word lasts forever!

6/23/96

40. The Book of Hope

Theme: The Bible

Bible Text: Everything that was written in the past was written to teach us. The Scriptures give us patience and encouragement so that we can have hope (Romans 15:4).

Preparation: Gather fairy tale books, cookbooks, comic books, coloring books, textbooks, and other books children will recognize. Be sure to include a dictionary and a Bible in your book collection.

The Message:

How many of you like to read? *Let children respond.* I love to read. In fact, I brought my book collection with me today. We can read so many different kinds of books. Let's play a little game with some of these books. I'll hold one up and you try to guess what kind of book it might be. *Hold up the dictionary.* What's in this book? *Let children respond.* Words! That's right! Thousands and thousands of words. People used words from this dictionary to write the rest of these books. Now, what's in this book? *Hold up various books and let the children try to guess what's inside. Be ready to offer help if necessary.*

Hold up the Bible. What's in this book? *Let children respond.* There are rules in this book and lots of stories. There's beautiful poetry, letters, and wonderful predictions about our future. Listen to what this book says about itself. *Read the text.*

This is a book about hope. Even when things go wrong, we have a reason to be happy. God will always love us, no matter what. Jesus died and rose again, and we can build our hope on him.

This book talks about Jesus a lot because this book is the Bible. The Bible is the book of hope, and it's a wonderful book to read any time.

I'm glad so many of you are reading or learning to read. *Point to your book collection.* I hope one day you'll read all these books and more. Books tell us about the wonderful world and people God has made. But there's one book we need to read every day—the Bible, God's book of hope.

41. What Are the Ten Commandments Like?

Theme: God's law

Bible Text: Deuteronomy 5:6-21

Preparation: Print the Ten Commandments on a large sheet of posterboard so everyone can see them. Choose a version of the Bible that children will understand. Put a baseball bat, a rope, a set of exercise weights, and a megaphone into a large bag or pillowcase. You can make your own megaphone by rolling a sheet of paper into a cone. If you don't have access to exercise weights, use a stack of books instead.

The Message:

What's a law? Can you think of some laws we have in our country? Do you have any laws at home? *Let children respond.*

Today we'll be talking about God's law. Who can name some of the Ten Commandments? *Let children respond.* The Ten Commandments are some of the most important laws in the Bible.

Do you know what the Ten Commandments are like? *Take out the baseball bat.* Some people say the Ten Commandments are like a baseball bat God uses to hit us over the head.

Take out the rope. Other people think the Ten Commandments are like a rope or chain God uses to tie us up and keep us from having any fun. *Loosely wrap the rope around a child.*

Take out the megaphone. Some people even think God uses the Ten Commandments to scold us.

But I think the Ten Commandments are like a set of weights.

Take out the weights and let kids take turns lifting them. We need to exercise our spiritual muscles in the same way we exercise the muscles in our bodies, and the Ten Commandments help us do that. We don't try to keep the Ten Commandments so God will love us. God already loves us, no matter what. We try to keep the Ten Commandments because we want to please God and be strong in our faith.

God gave us the Ten Commandments to help us strengthen our spiritual muscles. Let's read them together. *Lead children in reading the Ten Commandments from the poster you've prepared.*

42. Our Father Who Art in Heaven

Theme: Prayer

Bible Text: So when you pray, you should pray like this: "Our Father in heaven, may your name always be kept holy" (Matthew 6:9).

Preparation: The following seven children's messages are based on the Lord's Prayer as found in Matthew 6:9-13. Using the version of the Lord's Prayer your church uses in worship, print each part of the prayer on a sheet of posterboard to display during the message. For this week's message write "Our Father who art in heaven." During this series of messages, encourage the children to repeat what they've learned in previous weeks until they know the entire prayer.

The Message:

Jesus taught his disciples a very special prayer. We call this prayer the Lord's Prayer because our Lord Jesus made it up. For the next few weeks we're going to try to understand this prayer better. We'll learn a little bit each week, and by the time we're done we'll know the whole thing. Let's say the first part together. *Using the poster, repeat the words with the children.*

Stand up as you continue your message. Have you ever tried to talk with an adult who just wouldn't listen? Maybe you want to tell your mom something very important but she's talking with your dad. Does that ever happen to you? How do you get your mom's attention? *Let children respond.*

How do you feel when adults are too busy to listen? *Let children respond.* God is never too busy to hear our prayers. He's never too far over us, and he's always ready to listen to us. *Kneel down to kids' level.* That's why Jesus uses the word "Father" to describe God. God wants to be like the best daddy to us—the kind of dad who stoops down to look you in the eye and always has time to listen. *Stoop down and look a small child in the eye.*

God loves to hear our prayers. Let's pray the first part of Jesus' prayer one more time. *Repeat the words with the children.*

43. Hallowed Be Thy Name

Theme: Honoring God

Bible Text: So when you pray, you should pray like this: "Our Father in heaven, may your name always be kept holy" (Matthew 6:9).

Preparation: Write the phrase "Hallowed be thy name" on a sheet of posterboard and place it next to last week's poster. You'll need a book of baby names, nametags and pens, and one or two adult helpers. Write your name and its meaning on a nametag and wear it during the message.

The Message:

The last time we were together we talked about Jesus' special prayer. We learned that God is like a father to us. And God is always ready to listen to us when we pray. Jesus started his prayer by saying, "Our Father who art in heaven." The next part of the prayer goes like this: "Hallowed be thy name." Let's say the first two parts together. *Using the posters, repeat the words with the children.*

Names are very important. I brought a book along today that tells the meanings of names. *Point to your nametag.* My name is (presenter's name) and it means (meaning of name). Let's look up some of your names and see what they mean. While we're looking up names, my helpers will pass out nametags and pens. Write your name on your nametag and put it on the front of your shirt or dress.

Have your helpers assist the children who can't write. Look up several of the children's names and read their meanings to the group.

We can really hurt other people's feelings by making fun of their names. When people make fun of our names, it feels like they're making fun of us.

When we pray the words "Hallowed be thy name," we're promising God we'll respect his name. We're also saying we'll show how much we love God. If we say we love God, then our lives should show that, too.

Names are very important, and God's name is the most important name of all! Let's all wear our nametags today so everyone in our church will know our names.

44. Thy Kingdom Come, Thy Will Be Done
(Back-Seat Drivers)

Theme: Christian living

Bible Text: May your kingdom come and what you want be done, here on earth as it is in heaven (Matthew 6:10).

Preparation: Write the Bible text on a sheet of posterboard and place it next to the first two Lord's Prayer posters. Line up two rows of chairs facing the congregation. Each row should have three chairs. Ask two older children to help you, and rehearse the art of "back-seat driving" with them before the service.

The Message:

The next part of the Lord's Prayer is about doing what God wants us to do. Let's read it together. *Hold up today's poster and repeat the words with the children.* That was great! Now let's try the whole thing. *Read all three posters with the children.*

As God's people, we want to do what God wants us to do. But that's not always easy. First, we have to find out what God wants, and then we have to decide to do it.

It's just like driving a car. Now, I know none of you are old enough to drive a car. But have you ever been in a car with a "back-seat driver?" *Let children respond.* Let me show you what I mean. We'll pretend these two rows of chairs are a car. I'll be the driver and ask (name of child) and (name of another child) to sit next to me.

Who would like to sit in the back seat? *Choose three children, including your rehearsed back-seat drivers.*

Driver: Are we ready? All right, here we go, off to the store! Pretend to steer the car. I think I'll turn right at the corner.

Back-seat drivers: No, turn left! Stay straight ahead! Let's take the shortcut.

Driver: No, I'm turning right!

Back-seat drivers: You're going too fast. You're going too slow. Watch out for that car! Turn right! Turn left! *Your back-seat drivers may add additional comments.*

Now, what's the problem with back-seat drivers? *Let children respond.*

Someone has to be in charge of the car, and that someone is the driver. When everyone else is giving orders, it's very confusing and sometimes dangerous.

Sometimes we try to be back-seat drivers with God. We think we know what God's will should be and how his kingdom should come. We start telling God how to run this world. And that's very confusing and dangerous.

When we pray in the Lord's Prayer, "Thy kingdom come, thy will be done," we're telling God that we know he's in the driver's seat. We won't be back-seat drivers because God knows what's best for us!

Let's give (names of back-seat drivers) a hand for pretending to be such good back-seat drivers. *Lead the children and congregation in applauding your volunteers.*

80

45. Daily Bread

Theme: God provides.

Bible Text: Give us this day our daily bread (Matthew 6:11, KJV).

Preparation: Write the Bible text on a sheet of posterboard and place it next to the other Lord's Prayer posters. You'll also need a tablecloth to spread on the floor, paper plates, and a loaf of bread. Set the plates around the edge of the tablecloth and hide the bread nearby.

The Message:

I'd like to invite all of you to eat with me today. *Point to the tablecloth.* Find a place at the table and then we'll say a prayer before we eat. Let's use the Lord's Prayer. Be sure to notice the new part at the end. *Read today's text aloud for the children and then point to the posters and lead the children in saying the prayer.*

Hold up the loaf of bread. Look! We asked for bread, and God gave it to us. Let's eat!

Pass out the bread. I was thinking about having pizza or spaghetti, but Jesus taught us to pray for daily bread, not daily pizza or daily spaghetti. I don't usually get to eat a whole meal of just bread. Do any of you? *Let children respond.*

I'll bet if you ate a meal of bread every day, you might get tired of it. When the people of Israel were in the desert, they complained that they were hungry. So every day God gave them bread—just enough for that day. And you know what? They still complained! They wanted more than bread.

When we pray for daily bread, we ask God to give us just enough for today. We know God will be listening tomorrow to give us bread for that day.

But God gives us more than just bread. God gives us homes and families to take care of us. God provides us with a loving church and a wonderful nation. All those things come with daily bread.

God is the giver of all good things. And God hears and answers all our prayers. He'll give us everything we need and more!

46. Forgive Us Our Trespasses

Theme: Forgiveness

Bible Text: Forgive us for our sins, just as we have forgiven those who sinned against us (Matthew 6:12).

Preparation: Write the Bible text on a sheet of posterboard and place it next to the other Lord's Prayer posters. You'll need a basket of treats to share with the children.

The Message:

Look what I got this week. *Show the children your basket.* A basket of treats. Let's pretend someone gave these treats to me as a gift. I didn't have to buy them or earn them. Isn't that great? *Let children respond.*

Maybe I should share some of my treats with you. That would be a nice thing to do, wouldn't it? Do you all like treats? *Let children respond.*

Of course, if I gave all of you treats, there would be less for me. Maybe I shouldn't share with you. Maybe I should ask you to do something to earn the treats.

Of course, I didn't have to earn the treats. Someone just gave them to me. If I got the treats for free, I should probably give them to you for free, shouldn't I? *Let children respond.*

Sharing my treats is like today's part of the Lord's Prayer. *Read the text from today's poster.* Let's read all the parts we've learned so far. *Point to the posters and then lead the children in saying the prayer.* God shared his forgiveness by sending Jesus to die for us, and God wants us to share our forgiveness with others. But sometimes we forget about God's forgiveness. We get angry with others and don't want to forgive them. So Jesus teaches us to ask God to help us forgive others.

Because God shared his forgiveness with me, I can share my forgiveness with you. That calls for a celebration! Let's all give one another hugs of forgiveness. *Pause while children hug one another.* Would anyone like some treats to help celebrate? You don't have to earn them or buy them or deserve them. They're free—just like God's forgiveness.

Distribute the treats to the children.

47. Lead Us Not Into Temptation

Theme: Temptation

Bible Text: And lead us not into temptation, but deliver us from the evil one (Matthew 6:13, NIV).

Preparation: Write the Bible text on a sheet of posterboard and place it next to the other Lord's Prayer posters. You'll need a sports jersey and cap printed with a team logo.

The Message:

What's temptation? *Let children respond.* When we want to do something we're not supposed to do, that's temptation. We can be tempted by little things—like a fresh batch of cookies we're not supposed to eat until after supper. Or we can be tempted by big things like gossip or stealing. The next part of Jesus' prayer talks about temptation. Let's say it together. *Lead children in reading today's text from the poster.*

When people in Jesus' day prayed this part of the Lord's Prayer, they were asking God to help them keep following Jesus. They knew the devil would always tempt them to follow **him**, so they prayed for strength to resist that temptation. Imagine how terrible it would be to follow the devil instead of Jesus!

How many of you have a favorite sports team? *Let children respond.* My favorite team is the (name of sports team). In my spare time, I like to watch the (name of team). I know the names of their players, and I try to watch most of their games. I have a (name of team) T-shirt and cap. I'll keep on being a (name of team)'s fan whether they win or lose. I'm proud to wear this cap and shirt, especially when they're winning.

But if the (name of team) started losing lots of games, I might be tempted to leave my shirt in the drawer. I might even buy a shirt from the (name of rival team). We all like to support the winning team.

Our Lord Jesus is a real winner! He died on the cross for us and then rose again. Now that's winning. Only Jesus could win against death. But if things aren't going right, or if people are making fun of us because we're Christians, we might be tempted to stop following Jesus. That's when we need to pray, "Lead us not into temptation, but deliver us from evil." We're saying, "Help us to follow you, Lord Jesus, all the time—in good times and bad times. We're on your team forever!"

Before you go back to your seats, let's see if we can say the whole Lord's Prayer to this point. *Lead children in saying the Lord's Prayer using the posters you've set up.* Now let's all give three cheers for Jesus. We're on the winning team! *Lead children in cheers.*

48. The Kingdom, Power, and Glory Wave

Theme: Praise

Bible Text: He is the only God, the One who saves us. To him be glory, greatness, power, and authority through Jesus Christ our Lord for all time past, now, and forever. Amen (Jude 25).

Note: The phrase, "For thine is the kingdom, and the power, and the glory, forever" is not found in Matthew 6. However, its content is supported elsewhere in scripture, as noted above.

Preparation: Write the last part of the Lord's Prayer on a sheet of posterboard. Line up all the Lord's Prayer posters across the worship space so the children and the congregation can read them.

The Message:

For the past few weeks we've been learning about the Lord's Prayer. You've all done a great job of remembering the prayer so far. Today we're going to learn the last part. You won't find the last part of the Lord's Prayer in the book of Matthew. But Christians have spoken these words at the end of the Lord's Prayer for two thousand years. Let's say them together. *Using the poster, lead children in saying the last words of the Lord's Prayer.*

These words are our way of saying, "God, you're the greatest! Your name is holy. You give us daily bread and forgive our sins. We want to do your will forever. You're really great!"

Do you know what the last words of the Lord's Prayer remind me of? These words remind me of "the wave" we sometimes see at football games. Have you ever seen the wave? People all over the stadium stand up and sit down and wave their arms to cheer for their team.

We close the Lord's Prayer by cheering for God and everything God does for us. We don't have quite as many people as they do at football games, but let's try to do a "Kingdom, Power, and Glory Wave" anyway. We'll need to practice our wave a few times so we can teach it to the congregation.

Have the children crouch down in a single-file line across the front of the worship space. When I point to you, stand up, raise your arms over your head, and then sit down. Watch the person next to you so you'll be ready when your turn comes. Let's see if we can get a wave going. *Practice the wave two or three times before continuing.*

I think we're ready now. When we come to the last part of the Lord's Prayer, we'll do the "Kingdom, Power, and Glory Wave." Let's pray the prayer loudly so God and the whole congregation can hear us. Ready?

Let the children lead the congregation in praying the Lord's Prayer. When they come to the words, "For thine is the kingdom, and the power, and the glory, forever and ever, amen," have the children lead the congregation in a wave.

1/9/94
11/3/96

49. Where Does All the Money Go?

Theme: Stewardship

Bible Text: And God can give you more blessings than you need. Then you will always have plenty of everything—enough to give to every good work (2 Corinthians 9:8).

Preparation: You'll need an offering plate, offering envelopes, checks, a dollar bill, and a few coins. You'll also need a large box containing a Bible, cans of food, textbooks, pictures of the pastor or other church staff, a bottle of cleaning solution, and a hammer and nails. *This is a good message to use if your church has an annual stewardship Sunday.*

The Message:

How many of you have ever brought money to church to put into the offering? *Let children respond.* Every Sunday in church we pass an offering plate just like this one. *Hold up the offering plate.* As the plate passes down the rows, people can put in their offerings. Some people put their offering money in envelopes first. *Hold up an offering envelope.* Other people put their checks or money right into the plate. *Hold up the checks, the dollar bill, and the coins.*

Do you ever wonder where all that money goes? *Let children respond.* Let's ask (name of child) to put a dollar in the offering plate so we can see what happens to it. *Give the child a dollar to put into the offering plate.*

Our dollar bill is counted with all the other offerings and then put into the bank. *Put the offering plate into the box.*

Our church uses the money we put in the bank to help our missionaries tell other people about Jesus' love. *Take out the Bible, open it, and set it in front of the box.*

Our church uses the money we put in the bank to buy food for poor people. *Take out the cans of food and put them in front of the box.*

87

Our church uses the money we put in the bank to support Christian schools so young people can receive good Christian education. *Take out the textbooks and place them in front of the box.*

Our church uses the money we put in the bank to pay our pastor and other church workers. *Take out the pictures and put them in front of the box.*

Our church uses the money we put in the bank to help pay for our building and to keep it running smoothly. *Take out the bottles of cleaning solution, the hammer, and the nails, and place them in front of the box.*

So, where does all the money go? *Point to all the items in front of the box.* Here are just a few places. The money we put in the offering plate works in many different ways to tell people about Jesus.

Read the text. When we give our offerings, we're giving God back a small part of what he's given us. God can do great things with our offerings. Let's all remember to give this week.

50. Caution: Stewards at Work

Theme: Stewardship

Bible Text: The Parable of the Talents (Matthew 25:14-30).

Preparation: Photocopy the gift certificate handout on page 91 for each child. You'll also need 10 one-dollar bills. Ask one or two adults to help children who can't write fill out their gift certificates.

The Message:

Jesus once told a story about a man who went on a trip. Before he left, the man gave some money to his servants. He gave five dollars to his first servant. *Lay out five one-dollar bills for the children to see.* The first servant thought and thought about what he should do with his master's money. Finally he decided to put the money in the bank so it could earn more money. *Lay out five more one-dollar bills.*

When the man returned from his trip, he was so happy with his servant! "You have earned me five more dollars," he said. "Well done, good and faithful servant."

The man also gave two dollars to his second servant. *Lay out two one-dollar bills.* Maybe the second servant asked the first servant what he should do, because he too went out and earned more money. *Lay out two more one-dollar bills.* What do you think the man told that servant when he returned? *Let children respond.*

The man's third servant wasn't very brave. He didn't want to lose his master's money, so he hid the dollar his master had given him. *Hide a one-dollar bill under a seat cushion.* Now, what do you think the man told that servant? *Let children respond.* Not "well done," but "shame on you!" The third servant could have at least put the dollar into the bank instead of burying it.

Jesus tells us that story to teach us that God expects us to wisely use what he's given us. In the church we call that stewardship. Stewardship is taking care of something that belongs to someone else. Our world and

89

everything we have belongs to God.

God also gives each of us special gifts. We can use our gifts to serve God and others. I want each one of you to think of a special gift God has given you. *Give children a moment to think.* Have you all thought of something? *Let children respond.* Now I want you to think of a special person you know. Think of a way you can use your special gift this week to serve that special person you're thinking of. *Pass out the "I Have a Special Gift" handout, page 91.* Write your special gift and your special person on this gift certificate. *Have adult helpers work with children who haven't learned how to write.*

Remember to keep the promise you wrote on your gift certificate. It's fun to use the gifts God's given us!

I Have A Special Gift

This certificate entitles _____ to share my gift for

_____
special person

_____ this week.
special gift

_____
Child's signature

51. Back to Back
(A Children's Message for a Wedding)

Theme: Marriage

Bible Text: So there are not two, but one. God has joined the two together, so no one should separate them (Matthew 19:6).

Preparation: Discuss the children's message with the bride and groom.

Weddings are fascinating to children. They wonder why everyone is dressed so wonderfully, why there's so much celebration, and why there's such a mixture of laughter and tears. If the bride and groom agree, children can be included in the ceremony in a wonderful way.

The Message:

What a wonderful day this is for (name of bride) and (name of groom). Everyone is all dressed up in special clothes, and the music is so beautiful, and there are flowers everywhere. Do you know why this is such a special day? *Let children respond.*

We've all come to church today for (bride) and (groom)'s wedding, and that makes us very happy. Marriages are very special. God created (bride) and (groom), and he made them each happy as separate people. But one day they met each other. They became good friends, and one day they decided they loved each other so much they wanted to be together all the time. They promised to marry one another, and today they're promising to stay with each other for the rest of their lives.

When (bride) and (groom) promise to stay with each other forever, they'll face each other and hold hands. Let's ask them to do that now so we'll be prepared for that. *Give the bride's bouquet to a bridesmaid, and have the bride and groom face each other and hold hands.*

That's how (bride) and (groom) will look when they promise to stay with each other forever. They'll be together, and nobody will be between them.

But they can't keep standing there forever, can they? They both have to go to work, and they each have lots of things they like to do on their own. Let's ask them to stand back to back. *Position the bride and groom back to back, still holding hands.* (Bride) and (groom) are still joined together, but they're facing out. They can look out at all their friends. They can serve God in the world, but they're always connected to each other. Nobody's between them. And they can still face each other when they want to. *Turn the bride and groom to face each other.*

Marriage is God's way of joining a man and woman together so they can support and strengthen each other. We're so glad (bride) and (groom) have decided to get married. If you've known (bride) as a special friend, now you can have (groom) as a friend, too.

Listen to what Jesus said about marriage. *Read the text.* No one will ever come between (bride) and (groom). We're glad they're getting married. Let's show our love for them by giving them a big round of applause. *Lead the congregation in applause as children return to their seats.*

52. Love Is Like a Flowing Stream

(A Children's Message for a Wedding)

Theme: Love

Bible Text: Love never ends (1 Corinthians 13:8a).

Preparation: Discuss the children's message with the bride and groom. Fill a pitcher and a glass with water. Place a large bowl between the pitcher and the glass.

When single parents marry, children often worry that their love will be taken away by the new spouse. This message addresses children's fear that there won't be enough love left to go around.

The Message:

What a happy time this is for (name of bride) and (name of groom). God created (bride) and (groom), and today God has called them together to be husband and wife forever and ever. Today is especially exciting because (bride) and (groom) each have a family, so we'll be joining two families together, too.

I'd like to talk to the children for a minute about love. Sometimes when parents share their love with someone else, we worry that there won't be any love left for us. It's kind of like this glass of water. There's only so much water in this glass. If I gave a little bit to (name of child) and a little bit to (name of child) and a little bit to (name of child), I wouldn't have any water left for (names of other children).

Some children think if their mom shares her love with a new stepfather, she won't have any love left for them. Or if their dad gives all his love to their new stepmother, they won't get any.

But that's not the way the Bible thinks about love. *Read the text.* Love is like a never-ending stream. When a mom shares her love with a dad *(pour the water from the glass into the bowl)*, God gives her more love *(refill the glass from the pitcher)* to give to you. You can give some love back to your mom *(pour some of the water from the glass into the bowl)* or give love to your brothers and sisters *(pour the rest of the water in the glass into the bowl)*. Every time we think we're about to run out of love, God fills us right up again *(refill the glass from the pitcher)*.

God's love never ends. Jesus died on the cross to show us how much God loves us. God has more than enough love to go around for you and Mom and Dad and all of us.

We've all come today to celebrate (bride) and (groom)'s love for each other. But we've also come to thank God for his never-ending stream of love that fills us up forever.

INNOVATIVE RESOURCES FOR CHILDREN'S MINISTRY

5-Minute Messages for Children

Donald Hinchey

Captivate and challenge young listeners—with 52 Bible-based sermons just for them. Each creative message uses language kids readily understand—so you'll teach meaningful lessons on topics such as...

- ◆ God's love
- ◆ forgiveness
- ◆ faith
- ◆ putting God first

...and dozens of other topics. Plus, each talk uses involving activities to grab and hold kids' attention—so they'll remember the truths you present.

You'll also get seasonal ideas for helping children understand the meaning of...

- ◆ Advent
- ◆ Easter
- ◆ Christmas
- ◆ Pentecost

...and other important days. You'll use these lessons for children's moments in Sunday worship—or at camps, retreats, and other special events.

ISBN 1-55945-030-4 $8.99

Making Scripture Stick

Lisa Flinn & Barbara Younger

Discover 52 unforgettable Bible-verse adventures for children in grades 1–5. You'll use creative, hands-on learning techniques that draw kids into a world of imagination, discovery, and creative interaction. Bible verses come alive with these active, fun adventures as kids...

- ◆ make paper tambourines and use them to create a new song of praise (Psalm 150:4).
- ◆ run finger races and discuss the challenges that Christians face (Hebrews 12:1).
- ◆ blow bubbles and see that bubbles last an instant while God's love is forever (Psalm 90:2).
- ◆ make a foot-paint footprint banner and see how God watches their every step (Job 31:4).

The easy-to-prepare lessons feature a simple format, clear directions, inexpensive materials, reproducible handouts, and a wide variety of exciting activities. And follow-up discussions make the Bible messages stick!

ISBN 1–55945–093-2 $10.99

Quick Group Devotions for Children's Ministry

You'll discover 52 lively Bible-based devotions for elementary-age children...the best devotions used by 20 veteran children's workers from across the country. No dull sermonettes here, but active, experiential lessons that kids will enjoy *and* remember. Each touches on a Bible topic you want to teach like...

- ◆ complaining,
- ◆ God's love,
- ◆ honesty,
- ◆ prayer,
- ◆ friendship,
- ◆ overcoming temptation,

...and over 40 more! Plus, you'll find holiday devotions for New Year's Day, Valentine's Day, Easter, and Christmas. Perfect for Sunday school, children's church, vacation Bible school, day camps...any time children need to learn from the Bible.

ISBN 1-55945-004-5 $9.99

Available at your local Christian bookstore, or write: Group, Box 485, Loveland, CO 80539. Please add postage/handling of $4 for orders up to $15, $5 for orders of $15.01+. Colorado residents add 3% sales tax.